THE
REVOLVING
DOOR

Table of Contents

Introduction
Welcome to the Future of Employment

Welcome to this exciting journey into the world of Human Resource excellence! First, thank you, and I appreciate you for choosing my book to help you grow in your journey to becoming the expert on the employee life cycle at your place of employment. Your decision to dive into this adventure is super cool, and I'm right here to guide you through every step.

As Human Resource professionals, we often try to balance keeping it real and serving crucial information. Trust me; I've been there, too, and I understand the whole struggle. My aim? I want to help you find that sweet spot where you can be authentic, while picking up some killer human resource skills.

The Talent Shortage Reality Check

Before we dive headfirst into this journey, let's talk about a real-deal situation: we're facing a significant talent shortage. No sugar-coating it – there are way more job openings than there are qualified candidates to fill them. It's not just a minor hiccup; it's a talent scavenger hunt out there.

Think about it: holding onto your current crew is pure gold in a world where jobs pop up left and right. They're like the secret weapon to your company's success. Their skills, knowledge, and dedication – they're the real MVPs.

Let's dig into the stats for a second to get the whole picture. Recent surveys and studies show that the talent shortage is a global challenge. More than 70% of employers in the United States reported having difficulty finding and hiring skilled workers. It's not just a problem in one industry or region; it's a widespread issue.

But here's the kicker: this isn't just about numbers and statistics; it's about the impact on organizations like yours. When competing for a limited talent pool, it's not just about finding the right people; it's about keeping them, too. Losing top-notch employees can set your organization back, cost you valuable time and resources, and even impact your bottom line.

The Lowdown on Talent Retention

So, in this world of talent scarcity, keeping your rockstars isn't just a nice-to-have; it's a must-have. It's all about holding onto the talent you've got, helping them grow, and ensuring they stay fully committed and stoked. Talent retention isn't just fancy talk; it's your secret weapon for building rockstars and forward-thinking organizations that are ready to tackle whatever the future throws their way, will be able to conquer the world's talent shortage issues.

But let's not stop at the basics. Talent retention isn't just about preventing people from jumping ship; it's about creating an environment where they want to stay engaged and thrive. It's about turning your workplace into a place where employees don't just work; they flourish.

Why Talent Retention Rocks

Why does talent retention rock? Well, for starters, it's a significant cost-saver. When you lose an employee, it's more than just the time and effort spent on recruitment; it's also the lost knowledge, the disrupted workflows, and the training of new hires. It all adds up.

But beyond the financial benefits, talent retention is a game-changer for your company's culture. When your employees feel valued and appreciated and see opportunities for growth and advancement, they're more likely to be enthusiastic, motivated, and productive.

Talent retention also boosts your company's brand. It sends a clear message to the job market that your company is a great place where people want to stay. That, in turn, makes it easier to attract new talent.

I know what you might think: "Okay, this all sounds great, but how do I actually do it?" That's where this journey comes in. We're going to explore the strategies, the practices, and the insights that are shaping the employment landscape.

A Glimpse of What's Ahead

In the upcoming chapters, we'll dive deep into snagging top talent, check out how workplace vibes shift, and learn how to make your team grow and stick around. We will rock the tech-human dance, adapt to the crazy speed of change, and get your organization all prepped for the future.

We'll start by taking a closer look at attracting the right talent. We'll explore the concept of employer branding and how it can set you apart in a competitive market. Then, we'll move into the recruitment process, dissecting what it takes to bring in diverse and skilled individuals.

Once they're in the door, we'll talk about the onboarding process – how to ensure your new hires feel like part of the family from day one. We'll dive into learning and development, exploring how to keep your team growing and engaged.

We'll also chat about the tricky subject of performance management and rewards, ensuring everyone gets a fair shot.

Last but not least, we'll dive into the often-overlooked world of retaining your team and managing exits in a way that's aligned with your inclusion goals.

This isn't just theory talk; we're getting hands-on with real-world examples, pro tips, and stuff you can immediately implement. This isn't just a book; it's your backstage pass to shaping the future of how your organization rocks employment.

So, as we kick off our adventure into "The Future of Employment," brace yourself for a wild ride. The talent frontier is calling, and we will blaze the trail forward.

1

Talent Attraction

A winner is someone who recognizes their God-given talents, works their tail off to develop them into skills, and uses these skills to accomplish their goals.

– Larry Bird

Have you ever breezed past those corporate billboards on the highway, boldly proclaiming 'now hiring' or 'kickstart your career here'? They're like a coin with two sides, aren't they? Sometimes, you look at them and think, 'That place seems fantastic; I've heard some awesome buzz about them.' But there are moments when you might wonder, 'Hmm, that company appears desperate, and the grapevine isn't singing their praises.'

Ever wondered where your own company falls on that spectrum? Is it the kind of place everyone aspires to join, or do people roll with it because they haven't stumbled upon something better? If you find your company in the latter camp, it's time to flip the script. And even if your organization is already rockin' as a top-tier employer, there's always room for a little extra spice.

Building Your Dream Team

The talent attraction phase is like your grand opening to the job market. It's where the magic begins, where you cast your net to find the perfect candidates to join your team and help your organization thrive. But you're not just looking for anyone; you're aiming for the cream of the crop – the talent that'll take your company to new heights. So, let's break it down and see how you can make this phase rock.

Employer Branding: Painting Your Canvas

Imagine your organization as a canvas; employer branding is the paint that gives it color and character. This is where you create a story, a vibe, and an image that makes people say, "I want to work there." It's not just about the job; it's about your employees' culture, values, and experience.

Your employer brand is like the personality of your company. Is it fun and laid-back? Innovative and cutting-edge? Compassionate and community-focused? Whatever it is, make it shine! Authenticity is key here. Your brand should reflect who you really are.

Think about it this way: when someone sees your company's name, what should come to mind? Is it the cool tech startup with a ping-pong table in the breakroom or the eco-conscious organization with volunteer opportunities? That's your employer brand working its magic.

If you're anything like me and a solid 65% of people out there – the visual learners – you'll need to grab a pen and fast. It's not just for the workbook at the end of this chapter, but you'll also want it handy for some top-notch insights on employer branding I'm about to lay down. This isn't just chit-chat; it's the kind of info you can use immediately, trust me.

Take a moment to carefully consider each of these aspects of employer branding. Reflect on where your company stands in each section.

Some of you may rate all areas a perfect 5 out of 5. To make this more interesting, let's rank them from 1 to 6 instead. Assign a '1' to the area where your company excels the most, and mark the area needing the most improvement with a '6'. This approach will help you prioritize your focus and identify where your branding strategy truly shines and has room to grow.

_____ Employment Value Proposition

_____ Job Descriptions

_____ Sourcing Strategies

_____ Diversity and Inclusion

_____ Candidate Experience

_____ Social Responsibility

In the upcoming sections, we will delve deep into each aspect of your employer brand. Here's what I want you to do: circle the section you rated with a '6' – the one that needs the most improvement in your company. I'm not suggesting you skip over the other sections and jump straight to your lowest score. Each section is interconnected and vital in shaping a stellar employer brand. However, pay extra attention when you reach the section marked as a '6'. That's where I want you to focus your note-taking, as it's a key area for development in your company's employer brand journey to excellence.

Employment Value Proposition (EVP): What's in It for Them?

Let's discuss the deal you're offering your potential superstars – the Employment Value Proposition (EVP). It's like the perks of joining your squad. Consider it a win-win contract: You bring your A-game, and we'll give you these incredible rewards.

Your EVP is the combo of salary, benefits, culture, and growth opportunities that make candidates say, "Wow, I want in!" It's not just about the paycheck (although that's important); it's about the entire package. It could be flexible hours, remote work options, wellness programs, or career development paths.

Remember, your EVP should be irresistible. It's not just about attracting talent; it's about retaining it, too. So, ensure your employees will still love it after they've been with you for a while.

Job Descriptions: Crafting the Perfect Pitch

Imagine crafting a job description as if it's one of those captivating infomercials. You know, the ones that break down a product so effectively and speak directly to you, making you feel like you need to buy it. Remember that analogy – it's all about making the job sound irresistible, addressing the candidate directly, and highlighting every enticing detail. Now that you've got this picture and understand the approach, welcome to the talent attraction game. It's time to make your job descriptions so compelling that top candidates can't wait to apply.

But here's the deal: be honest and specific. No one likes a bait-and-switch. If the job involves less glamorous tasks, it's okay to mention them. Authenticity goes a long way in building trust with candidates.

Oh, and use language that's easy to understand. Skip the corporate jargon and buzzwords. Keep it clear, concise, and engaging. Imagine you're talking to a friend about the job – what would you say?

Sourcing Strategies: Where to Find the Gems

Now that you've got your job descriptions ready, it's time to shout them from the rooftops or, in this case, on the right platforms. Sourcing strategies are all about finding those hidden gems in the talent pool.

You've got options here. Job boards, social media, networking events, and employee referrals are all in play. But remember, it's not just about casting a wide net; it's about throwing it in the right places.

Tech forums and LinkedIn might be your go-to spots if you're looking for tech whizzes. If you need creative minds, check out portfolios and creative industry events. Your sourcing strategy should align with the skills and personalities you're seeking.

Think of it like fishing. You don't catch marlins in a pond, right? You go where the marlins hang out. The same goes for finding top talent.

Diversity and Inclusion: Welcoming All-Stars from Every Sport

Diversity and inclusion are not just buzzwords but heartbeats of a thriving workplace. It's not just about attracting talent; it's about drawing diverse Talent from all walks of life.

Why does it matter? Well, diverse teams bring fresh perspectives, innovative ideas, and unique experiences. It's like having a blend of colors in your palette – you can create a masterpiece.

How do you make diversity and inclusion part of your talent attraction phase? Start by removing biases in your job descriptions and recruiting process. Encourage diverse candidates to apply. And create a workplace culture that celebrates differences.

Remember, it's not just about hitting quotas; it's about creating a space where everyone feels valued and can bring their whole selves to work.

Candidate Experience: Roll Out the Red Carpet

Okay, you've got candidates lining up – now, it's time to roll out the red carpet. Candidate experience is like the warm welcome at a five-star hotel. You want candidates to feel valued and appreciated throughout the entire process. I want to share a story exemplifying why creating an outstanding candidate experience is crucial.

Have you ever been to a DoubleTree hotel? If you have, you know they make some of the best cookies in the world (Sorry, Mom). Sure, calling them 'the best in the world' is an exaggeration, but they are delicious. I remember my first stay at a DoubleTree – I kept heading down to the front desk to grab more cookies. I must've eaten enough for ten families! The combination of those amazing cookies and their fantastic service made such an impression that now, whenever I travel, I always look for a DoubleTree. I've even raved about it to my friends and family, especially letting them know about those incredible cookies.

And that's precisely how you want people to feel about your candidate experience. Create something remarkable, and people will talk about it. They'll share their stories with friends and family. And do you know what happens then? You start attracting the best kind of applicants: referrals. And the best part? Referrals don't cost you a thing. That's the power of a great experience. Now, let's dive into the rest of this section and see how you can replicate this effect.

The first thing you want to do to improve the candidate experience is start with clear communication. Let candidates know what to expect at every stage. Nobody likes surprises in a job hunt.

And be respectful of their time. Please don't keep them waiting for weeks; it's like leaving a VIP guest in the lobby too long. Streamline your process and give timely feedback.

Lastly, gather feedback from candidates. What did they love about your process, and where could you improve? Their insights are pure gold for refining your talent attraction strategy.

Social Responsibility: More Than Just Profits

Social responsibility might not be the first thing that comes to mind in talent attraction, but it's becoming increasingly important to job seekers. Candidates want to work for organizations that give back and care about their impact on society and the environment.

It's like choosing between two restaurants: one serves excellent food, and the other serves great food and supports a local charity. Most people would pick the second one.

So, if your organization is involved in social responsibility initiatives, flaunt it! Let candidates know that by joining your team, they'll be part of something bigger – positively impacting the world.

Competitive Analysis: What Are the Others Up To?

Time to put on our detective hats and do some competitive analysis. What are other organizations in your industry offering regarding compensation, benefits, and workplace culture? You don't want to be caught off guard when a candidate says, "Well, your competitor is offering me this…"

Being aware of the competition is crucial for staying ahead in the game. It's similar to understanding other players' strategies in a game, allowing you to adjust and refine your approach. This ensures your Employment Value Proposition (EVP) truly stands out. But remember, this doesn't mean you should immediately rush to your management team and insist on raising salaries to compete. Instead, take a comprehensive look at your total rewards package. Conduct thorough research – not everyone is primarily motivated by salary.

Consider who you're trying to attract to your company. For instance, if the average age of your employees is over 35, they might be more interested in aspects like healthcare, retirement plans, and other long-term benefits. Conversely, if your workforce is predominantly under 25, they might focus more on immediate financial compensation. In this case, you should adjust elements like 401k contributions or healthcare coverage to appeal more to this talent market demographic.

Always remember that it's not just about matching what your competitors offer; it's about going one step further. Aim to provide something unique that sets you apart, making your organization the one candidate is eager to join.

Talent Analytics: Data-Driven Decisions

Last but not least, let's talk about talent analytics. This is where you allow data to be your guide. Measure the effectiveness of your talent attraction strategies and make data-driven decisions.

Are your job postings getting clicks? Which sourcing channels are bringing in the most candidates? What's the conversion rate from application to hire? These are the questions talent analytics can answer.

By analyzing the data, you can refine your approach. A specific job board isn't delivering results, or your candidate experience needs some tweaking. Talent analytics helps you see where you're shining and where you need a polish.

Unlocking Talent Attraction Excellence: Google's Inspirational Journey

When we talk about mastering the art of talent attraction, one company that truly shines is Google. It's not just about Google's colossal size and renowned reputation; it's about the exceptional talent attraction strategies from which any organization, irrespective of its dimensions or budget, can draw inspiration.

Google's voyage into the world of talent attraction begins with an unwavering commitment to employer branding that vividly portrays its distinctive corporate culture. Often hailed as a hub of innovation, creativity, and inclusivity, Google weaves these threads into its branding tapestry. Through captivating campaigns like "Life at Google," the company not only shares the stories of its employees but also spotlights its community engagement initiatives and showcases the extraordinary perks that set it apart. The result? A brand that consistently graces the zenith of lists featuring the "Best Places to Work," attracting millions of job applications year after year.

Beyond mere imagery lies Google's secret weapon—its Employment Value Proposition (EVP). While competitive compensation and an array of benefits certainly contribute to the allure, Google's EVP transcends the realm of material gains. It champions professional growth, fosters a culture of continuous learning, and offers the golden ticket to engage in groundbreaking projects. The outcome? An awe-inspiring employee retention rate, with many choosing to sculpt enduring careers within the Google ecosystem.

Google's approach to job descriptions is refreshingly candid and inclusive. In a world often cluttered with convoluted jargon, Google opts for straightforward language that resonates with candidates. Yet, what truly sets Google apart is its unswerving dedication to diversity and inclusion. These pillars are prominently featured in the company's job postings, delivering a resounding message of an open, welcoming, and all-embracing workplace. This, in turn, fuels Google's ability to draw in diverse Talent.

At Google, diversity and inclusion aren't empty buzzwords; they're etched into the fabric of the company's identity. Google has set ambitious diversity goals and established robust resources to support employee resource groups, mentorship programs, and initiatives to attract underrepresented

Talent. Their commitment extends beyond their walls as Google actively champions external diversity organizations and provides grants to nonprofit entities that foster diversity and inclusion in the tech industry.

Google's remarkable journey in talent attraction serves as a beacon of inspiration. It underscores that a meticulously crafted employer brand, a compelling EVP, candid and inclusive job descriptions, and an unwavering commitment to diversity and inclusion can exponentially amplify an organization's ability to attract top-tier Talent. While Google is a more prominent company, its principles can be readily embraced by organizations of all sizes, igniting the spark to create an alluring employer brand and magnetizing the right Talent to fuel innovation and growth.

As we wrap up this journey through talent attraction, you've gained knowledge about building a magnetic employer brand, from understanding your EVP to embracing diversity and inclusivity, just like Google. You've explored the art of crafting compelling job descriptions and the significance of a positive candidate experience. Now, it's time to put these concepts into action.

Workbook #1

Welcome to the first workbook in 'The Revolving Door.' The workbooks are designed to help you assess and enhance each phase of the employee life cycle at your organization. Please follow the directions carefully and have fun with your findings, too.

Section 1: Talent Attraction

On a scale of 1 to 5, how well do you think your company attracts top-tier talent?

- ☐ 1 (Not at all)
- ☐ 2 (Below Average)
- ☐ 3 (Average)
- ☐ 4 (Above Average)
- ☐ 5 (Excellent)

Advice

If you rated your company below 4, consider focusing on improving your talent attraction strategies.

Gap Analysis

Identify Weaknesses: Begin by identifying the specific areas where your talent attraction strategies are falling short. This could include aspects of employer branding, EVP, job descriptions, or candidate experience.

Benchmark Against Competitors: Look at what your competitors are doing to attract talent. Are there any strategies or benefits they offer that you can learn from and incorporate into your own approach?

Seek Employee Feedback: Talk to your current employees to understand their perspective on your company's attractiveness as an employer. Their insights can be valuable in identifying areas for improvement.

Gap Analysis

Conduct Culture Assessment: Conduct an internal assessment to understand your company's true culture and values. Ensure that your employer brand accurately reflects these aspects.

Employee Stories: Encourage current employees to share their stories and experiences working at your company. Authentic employee testimonials can help showcase your culture.

Consistency is Key: Ensure that your employer brand is consistent across all communication channels, from your website to social media profiles. Consistency builds trust.

Section 2: Employer Branding

How would you describe your company's employer brand in a few words?

_____

_____

_____

Advice

If your employer brand isn't authentic, work on aligning it with your company's true culture and values.

Section 3: Employment Value Proposition (EVP)

On a scale of 1 to 5, how compelling and competitive is your EVP?

- ☐ 1 (Not at all)
- ☐ 2 (Below Average)
- ☐ 3 (Average)
- ☐ 4 (Above Average)
- ☐ 5 (Excellent)

<u>Analyze</u>

What does your Employment Value Proposition (EVP) offer to potential employees?

<u>Advice:</u>

If your EVP isn't competitive, consider enhancing the package to attract and retain top talent.

Salary & Benefits   **Professional Growth**   **Wellness Programs**

<u>Gap Analysis</u>

Targeted Platforms: Use the right platforms for job postings to target your desired candidates effectively and tailor your approach for specific roles.

Employee Referrals: Boost employee referrals through incentives to identify candidates who align with your company culture.

Networking: **Attend industry events and conferences for effective networking and building personal connections with potential candidates.**

Section 4: Sourcing Strategies

Are your sourcing strategies aligned with the skills and personalities you're seeking in candidates Yes or No? Explain why?

<u>Advice</u>

Optimize your sourcing strategies to target the right candidates effectively.

Section 5: Diversity and Inclusion

How diverse is your company's workforce currently?

<u>Analyze and Advice</u>

What steps does your company take to promote diversity and inclusion in its talent attraction process?

★ **Enhance diversity and inclusion efforts to tap into a wider pool of talent.**

Section 6: Social Responsibility

Does your company engage in social responsibility initiatives? If yes, how does it communicate this to potential candidates?

Gap Analysis

Communication: Maintain clear and prompt communication with candidates at every stage of the hiring process. Inform them of timelines and expectations.

Efficiency: Streamline your hiring process to minimize delays. Respect candidates' time and provide feedback promptly.

Personalization: Personalize the candidate experience by tailoring interactions to individual needs and preferences.

Section 7: Candidate Experience

How would you rate your company's candidate experience, from initial contact to hiring decision?

- ☐ 1 (Poor)
- ☐ 2 (Below Average)
- ☐ 3 (Average)
- ☐ 4 (Above Average)
- ☐ 5 (Excellent)

Gap Analysis

Honesty and Clarity: Review your job descriptions for honesty and clarity. Remove any exaggerated language or vague descriptions. Candidates appreciate straightforwardness.

Highlight Unique Aspects: Highlight what makes your company and the role unique. Mention any exciting projects, opportunities for growth, or company culture aspects.

Avoid Jargon: Keep language simple and avoid corporate jargon. Make sure the job descriptions are easily understandable to a wide range of candidates.

Section 8: Job Descriptions

How would you rate your company's job descriptions in terms of clarity and honesty?

- ☐ 1 (Not clear and honest)
- ☐ 2 (Somewhat clear and honest)
- ☐ 3 (Moderately clear and honest)
- ☐ 4 (Very clear and honest)
- ☐ 5 (Extremely clear and honest)

2
Recruitment

Your human talent is your most important talent.

– Carla Harris

Welcome to Chapter 2! If you've followed along, you know we're all about mastering the employee life cycle. We've laid the groundwork with 'Talent Attraction,' guess what? We're now diving into the exciting world of 'Recruitment.'

Think of the 'Recruitment' phase like this: you've got a dating app on your phone and swiping left and right. That's Talent Attraction - the initial attraction game. But now, it's time for the real deal and for 'Recruitment.'

Imagine this phase as the part where you've matched with someone interesting, and you're getting to know each other better. It's like a first date. In the business world, we call that the 'interview phase.' Here, both parties - you and your potential candidate - check each other out, ask questions, and see if there's chemistry.

In the dating world, if you go on too many dates without committing, you might scare your potential partner away, right? Well, the same goes for the hiring process. We want to keep our candidates manageable. So, we've got to strike the right balance.

Eventually, in the dating world, you might decide, 'Hey, let's make this official.' That's your 'offer' phase, where you pop the big question. In the employee life cycle, you extend an offer to a candidate who has aced the interviews. Then comes the onboarding, where you officially welcome them into your corporate family.

As we venture further into this chapter, consider it your guide to becoming a pro in 'Talent Acquisition.' We'll uncover strategies, tactics, and hacks that will help you find the perfect match for your team and make them excited to join your squad.

So, grab your metaphorical dating app for recruitment because things are about to get interesting. Swipe on 'Talent Acquisition,' and let's embark on this exciting journey together!"

Job Vacancy Identification: Timing is Everything

The first step in successful recruitment is identifying the need for a new employee. It's about assessing your preferences (organization's needs) and recognizing when you're open to new connections.

Timing is crucial in the world of recruitment. Knowing when you're ready for a new relationship is essential, as in dating. Imagine scrolling through profiles on a dating app. You would only do it if you were open to connecting. Similarly, as an organization, you need to assess your readiness to start the recruitment journey. Are you prepared to invest time and effort in finding the right match for your team?

Job Posting and Advertising: Creating an Appealing Profile

Crafting job postings and advertisements is akin to creating an appealing profile. You want to make a great first impression and catch the eye of potential candidates. Use language that resonates with your target audience and showcases your company's personality (culture).

Your job posting should be like a well-crafted profile highlighting your organization's best features. It should clearly convey the role's responsibilities, qualifications, and expectations. Much like a dating profile, you want to ensure your job posting represents your organization authentically. Honesty is critical, as attracting candidates who align with your culture and values is essential for long-term compatibility.

Sourcing and Candidate Pool: Active Search for Connections

Now, let's talk about sourcing and building your candidate pool. Think of it as actively seeking individuals who catch your eye and have the potential to be great matches.

In dating, actively searching for potential partners is a common practice. You may attend social events, join clubs, or even use dating apps to connect with people who share your interests. Similarly, in recruitment, sourcing involves actively seeking individuals who may not be actively looking for a job but have the skills and qualifications your organization needs.

Like in dating, where you actively seek people who align with your interests, sourcing candidates is about proactively identifying individuals who possess the qualities and skills your organization values. It's about expanding your network and engaging with potential matches even when there isn't an immediate need.

Resume Screening: Selecting the Best Matches

As you receive applications and resumes, it's time to sift through them. This is where you decide which profiles (resumes) catch your eye and match your preferences.

Think of resume screening as reviewing a stack of potential matches' profiles. You're seeking specific qualities and attributes that align with your organization's needs.

In the dating world, once you've connected with someone, you review their profile to determine if they're a potential match. Similarly, in recruitment, reviewing resumes is the initial step in assessing whether a candidate could be a good fit for your organization.

Interviews: Getting to Know Each Other

Ah, interviews – the beating heart of the recruitment process, where candidates are met face-to-face (or virtually). Before delving into this crucial phase, let's remember the saying, "retention starts with selection." What does that mean exactly? It underscores the significance of choosing the right candidate to improve overall retention and break the metaphorical 'Revolving Door'. Selecting the ideal candidate is very important to breaking the quick and endless cycle. Thus, during interviews, it's vital to ask the right questions, jot down their responses meticulously, observe their body language, and trust your instincts regarding any red flags, as they often prove to be accurate. Now, let's go further into the interview phase of talent acquisition, also known as recruitment.

Interviews are your opportunity to get to know candidates better. It's a chance to have a conversation, ask questions, and gauge whether there's a genuine connection.

Imagine going on a first date with someone you've been chatting with on a dating app. The conversation flows, and you start getting to know each other better. You ask your date about interests, experiences, and aspirations. Similarly, during interviews, you aim to uncover more about the candidate. You inquire about their skills, experiences, and motivations. The interview is your chance to explore whether there's a mutual connection and alignment with your organization's culture and values.

Skills Assessment: Discovering Hidden Talents

Sometimes, it's essential to dig deeper and assess specific skills. We'll explore when it's the right time to utilize skill assessments in the recruitment process.

Skills assessments help you uncover strengths and weaknesses that may take time to be apparent. In the dating analogy, this phase is like discovering hidden talents and interests that can contribute to a deeper connection.

Just as in dating, where you may discover shared hobbies or interests that strengthen your bond, skills assessments in recruitment reveal talents and proficiencies that can enhance a candidate's suitability for a role. It's an opportunity to delve deeper into a candidate's skill set and ensure they have the necessary capabilities to excel.

Reference Checks: Verifying Compatibility

Reference checks can be a valuable tool, especially when you're in between two strong candidates. However, they can also slow down the interview process. We'll discuss when and how to utilize reference checks effectively.

Reference checks help verify a candidate's compatibility with your organization. Much like seeking input from friends or acquaintances about someone you're dating, reference checks provide insights into a candidate's past performance and compatibility with your organization's values and requirements.

In the dating world, when you're uncertain about someone you're getting to know, you may seek opinions from people who know them well. Similarly, reference checks serve as a way to gather information from individuals who have worked closely with the candidate, helping you assess their compatibility with your organization.

Background Verification: Building Trust

Background verification is about confirming that the information provided aligns with reality. Background verification ensures the integrity of your hiring process. Like in dating, where trust is crucial for building a solid relationship, background verification is essential for establishing trust between your organization and the candidate.

Imagine going on a date and realizing the person you've been talking to has yet to be entirely honest about their background or past experiences. It can erode trust and make you question the authenticity of the connection. Similarly, background verification ensures that a candidate's information aligns with their actual history and qualifications. It's a step that helps build trust and confidence in the candidate's suitability for the role.

Offer Negotiation: Sealing the Deal

Finally, imagine you've been on several successful coffee dates and are ready to take the next step. You decide to make things official – akin to extending an offer to a candidate. It's a crucial phase in the employment process, as both parties need to agree on the terms of the relationship.

Offer negotiation is like discussing the terms of exclusivity. It's the time to talk about compensation, benefits, and expectations. Open and honest communication is critical to ensuring both parties are on the same page.

In the world of recruitment, the offer is a significant milestone. It signifies that you and the candidate see potential in this relationship and are ready to move forward. After you have made things official you enter into the onboarding and development phase. In the next chapter we'll explore nurturing solid employee-employer relationships. We will also discuss open communication, mutual respect, and shared values. This will pave the way for a successful partnership. It's about creating an environment where both parties can thrive and grow together."

HubSpot - Pioneering Recruitment Excellence

HubSpot, the rockstar of inbound marketing and sales software, is a brilliant example of how to nail recruitment in style. Even though HubSpot is a corporate heavyweight, its playbook is open for all to draw inspiration from, regardless of your organization's size or budget.

Let's break down HubSpot's recruitment groove:

At HubSpot, they're not sitting around waiting for job openings to pop up like mushrooms after rain. Nope, they're ahead of the game. Their recruitment squad actively scouts for top Talent and keeps tabs on potential future job slots. It's all about building relationships with potential candidates and ensuring a steady flow of Talent even before the seats are empty.

HubSpot doesn't do boring job listings. Their job descriptions are like a breath of fresh air. They infuse life into those words, making them resonate with their target crowd. They flaunt creativity and innovation in their ads, drawing in candidates who vibe with their culture.

They don't just wait for resumes to flood in; they're actively hunting Talent. From rocking industry events to mingling with potential candidates on social media, their pool has been stocked. And they maintain a talent pool, ready to dive in when the time is right.

It's not just about qualifications; it's about cultural fit. HubSpot looks for candidates whose values groove with theirs. They want folks who have the skills and share the mindset to ride the innovation wave.

HubSpot's interviews are legendary. They're not your run-of-the-mill Q&A sessions. They're challenging, they're insightful. They assess technical skills, sure, but they also freak out if you click with the team and vibe with their culture. It's like a jam session where they're looking for the right notes to create the perfect harmony.

While only some roles need a skills assessment, HubSpot is open to using them when necessary. For the tech gigs, they might throw in coding tests or hands-on projects. It's like a guitarist tuning their strings before hitting the stage – it ensures everyone's in sync.

HubSpot believes in dotting their i's and crossing their t's. They value reference checks as a final validation step. It's like getting your friend's thumbs-up before committing to a blind date.

They want to make sure what's on paper matches reality. No smoke and mirrors here. It's like making sure that killer guitar solo you heard in a recording is just as epic live on stage.

HubSpot isn't into playing hardball when it comes to negotiations. They aim for a win-win where both sides groove to the same beat. It's like ensuring the band and venue are happy before the concert.

HubSpot's talent attraction strategies are like a well-tuned guitar solo – smooth, impressive, and unforgettable. They've nailed it by aligning their recruitment with their values and culture. So, whether your organization is a titan or a startup, you can riff off their methods to attract and retain top Talent.

Let's move on to Workbook #2, where we'll break down these strategies and help you fine-tune your recruitment game. Get ready to rock the recruitment stage, just like HubSpot.

Workbook #2

Section 1: Sourcing and Candidate Pool:

Here is a compilation of the top 15 candidate sourcing channels for recruiters. We recommend discussing these sources with your recruitment team to determine how many of them your company currently utilizes. This conversation should also explore the reasons behind your company's usage of these channels and any factors influencing why certain channels are not used.

- ☐ LinkedIn
- ☐ Indeed
- ☐ Glassdoor
- ☐ Monster
- ☐ CareerBuilder

- ☐ Employee referral
- ☐ Career pages
- ☐ Job fairs
- ☐ Meetup groups
- ☐ SHRM

- ☐ ZipRecruiter
- ☐ Alumni networks
- ☐ Social media platforms
- ☐ Recruiting agencies
- ☐ College and university career services

Gap Analysis

In this section write down the sourcing channels that your team does not currently use, and provide the reasons behind their decisions. After completing this step, take some time to research each unused sourcing channel to explore potential solutions that could overcome any obstacles preventing your team from utilizing them. This exercise is not meant to prove your team wrong but to discover tools and strategies that can grant them access to a broader pool of candidates and simplify their recruitment process. Keep in mind that your team is busy with recruiting and interviews, so they might not have had the opportunity to research alternative methods to make these sourcing channels work for them.

Section 2: Resume Screening

In this exercise you will be reviewing the resume screening process and looking at a resume that has been submmited for a forklift operator job at a warehouse.

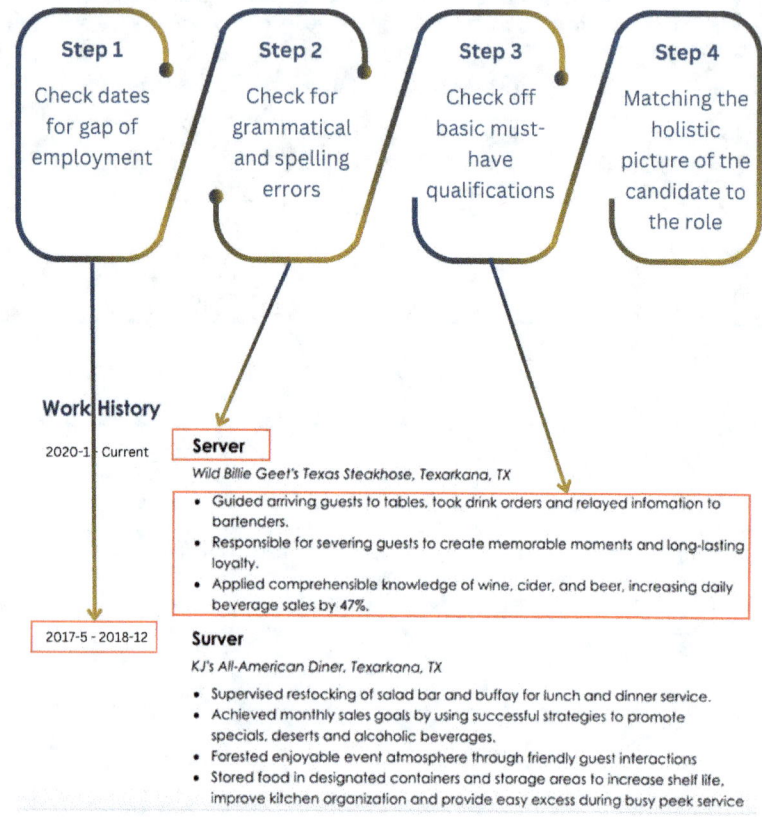

Step 1
Check dates for gap of employment

Step 2
Check for grammatical and spelling errors

Step 3
Check off basic must-have qualifications

Step 4
Matching the holistic picture of the candidate to the role

Work History

2020-1 - Current

Server
Wild Billie Geet's Texas Steakhose, Texarkana, TX
- Guided arriving guests to tables, took drink orders and relayed infomation to bartenders.
- Responsible for severing guests to create memorable moments and long-lasting loyalty.
- Applied comprehensible knowledge of wine, cider, and beer, increasing daily beverage sales by 47%.

2017-5 - 2018-12

Surver
KJ's All-American Diner, Texarkana, TX
- Supervised restocking of salad bar and buffay for lunch and dinner service.
- Achieved monthly sales goals by using successful strategies to promote specials, deserts and alcoholic beverages.
- Forested enjoyable event atmosphere through friendly guest interactions
- Stored food in designated containers and storage areas to increase shelf life, improve kitchen organization and provide easy excess during busy peek service

Overview

Step 1: There is a gap of employment from December 2018 to January 2020. I am a firm believer of life does happen, but these are red flags that need to be investigated as the events that may have occurred during this gap may be a deciding factor in interviewing or even hiring this individual if they make it to the offer stage.

Step 2: Grammatical errors are minor red flags, but if you have a position where the individual needs to have great attention to detail like an accountant you might want to take this lack of attention to detail into consideration.

Step 3: Remember this scenario was based off of a warehouse forklift driver. This person does not have any of the basic must have qualifications to even be considered for this position.

Step 4: The final step is putting it all together making sure the individual has all of the necesary qualifications and their resume is well put together with no concerning employment gaps. If you can check the boxes on all of these things I would move this candidate to the interview portion of your process.

Section 3: Interviews

Develop a set of interview questions that reveal a candidate's alignment with your organization's culture and values.

Instructions:

Core Values Reflection
List your organization's top 5 core values or cultural attributes. For each value, write a brief description of why it is important to your organization.

Question Development
Based on the core values listed above, develop at least one open-ended interview question per value that aims to uncover a candidate's compatibility. Ensure these questions encourage candidates to share experiences or viewpoints that reflect their alignment with these values.

Scenario-Based Questions
Create a hypothetical scenarios that could occur within your organization. For your scenario, develop a question asking how the candidate would respond, focusing on actions that demonstrate alignment with your organization's values.

Behavioral Questions
Formulate a behavioral questions asking candidates to describe past work experiences where they demonstrated qualities or actions that align with your core values.

Value Alignment Discussion
Draft 1-2 questions that invite candidates to discuss how they see their personal values and work style aligning with your organization's culture and mission.

Example Questions:

Core Value: Team Collaboration

Question: *"Can you share an example of a time when you had to work closely with a team under tight deadlines? How did you ensure effective collaboration and communication?"*

Scenario: Handling Conflict

Question: *"Imagine you're working on a project and there's a disagreement within the team about the direction to take. How would you approach this situation while maintaining respect for all team members' viewpoints?"*

Behavioral: Adaptability

Question: *"Tell us about a time when you had to adapt quickly to changes in project goals or organizational priorities. What was your approach, and what was the outcome?"*

Value Alignment: Innovation

Question: *"Our organization values innovative thinking. Can you discuss a situation where you had to think outside the box to solve a problem? What was the challenge, and what was your solution?"*

Completion
After developing your questions, review them with your team to ensure they accurately reflect the intended core values and are likely to elicit informative responses. Consider conducting mock interviews with team members to refine question phrasing and determine the effectiveness of each question in gauging candidate compatibility.

3
Onboarding

If you don't care, your customer never will.

– Marlene Blaszczyk

These wise words by Marlene Blaszczyk resonate deeply in customer service and how we treat our colleagues and team members. This sentiment becomes abundantly clear when we examine my two contrasting onboarding experiences within the professional world.

I've got this vivid memory of witnessing an awful onboarding experience back in the day when I was starting out. I'd already been at that company for a few months, but when this new team member, John, walked in all pumped up, things took a turn for the worse.

Here's the kicker – this wasn't a one-time thing. They'd pulled the same stunt on me when I first joined, but I was green back then and didn't know any better. So, let me spill the beans on what went down with John.

They basically left him stranded at his desk for hours. No computer, no warm welcome, not even a heads-up that someone was supposed to show him the ropes. It's like they straight-up forgot he existed. You could cut the frustration and boredom in the air with a knife.

By lunchtime, John had enough, he scribbled a note on his empty desk and made a break for it. And here's the gut punch – they wouldn't even cough up some cash for his wasted day. Ouch, right?

That right there, my friend, is a prime example of "unprofessional." It's a big, flashing warning sign that a lousy onboarding process can make even the most eager person want to hit the road.

As time passed, these vibes spread to other parts of the company, like how they treated their existing crew. In ten short months, I had to make the "tough decision" to part ways with that company.

But hold on, let me switch gears and talk about my onboarding experience at a different company – a game-changer regarding how they roll out the red carpet for new team members.

Stepping into that front lobby felt like a warm hug from day one. Smiles, high-fives, the whole nine yards. My new colleagues made me feel like I'd joined a big, awesome family.

Picture this: remember when you were a kid walking through the front door, and everyone shouted "SURPRISE!" at your birthday party? Your buddies are all around, giving you high-fives and hugs. And then you spot a table piled with gifts. That's the kind of vibe you want to recreate.

Back to my first day – After greeting me, my new team showed me around again and then took me to my office/desk. My desk was decorated with company swag and fabulous gifts that oozed their unique style. They had a card that was signed by everyone in my department and loaded with kind words.

And to top it off? My computer was all set up and ready to go. No waiting around, no tech hiccups. They'd pulled out all the stops to make my first day smooth and productive.

But the cherry on top as a company is to make sure they have a lunch, whether you take them to lunch or order lunch for their team and have them eat together in the break room. You want to make sure their first day is smooth and easy. Ensure they don't feel alone on that first day by not giving them time alone. That may sound bad because we all need our space, but they will have plenty of alone time in the future.

To finish my story, my team took me to lunch. And it was a blast. We went to this sweet restaurant nearby. It wasn't just about the grub; we laughed, swapped stories, and got to know each other. You could tell they didn't just value my skills; they wanted me to be part of their team.

Looking back on that killer onboarding experience, I'm stoked to say I'm still with that company today. It's a rock-solid reminder of how a top-notch onboarding process sets the stage for an incredible journey in the workplace. It's like the secret sauce for long-lasting success. And you know what? Experiences like these make team members think twice before packing their bags. They remember how great that ride was and know only some companies can pull it off. So, they're more likely to stick around, hash things out, and make it work.

Now, let's take a look into the first month of an employee's journey, exploring the stages of Pre-Onboarding, Orientation and Induction, Training and Development, and Socialization and Integration. These pivotal stages show your commitment to their well-being and lay the groundwork for a successful and fulfilling ride within your organization.

Pre-Onboarding (Before the First Day)

Now that your new hire has successfully navigated the rigorous selection process, accepted your offer, and eager for their first day at their new job, the excitement is palpable. You want them to know that even before they step through the office door, the Pre-Onboarding stage is where you set the stage for the entire employee journey. It's a phase where, as an HR professional, you have a unique opportunity to guide them in demonstrating commitment and care right from the beginning.

Imagine this scenario: The new team member, fresh off the excitement of accepting a job offer, receives a package at their doorstep. Inside, they find a beautifully wrapped gift, carefully selected to make them feel valued and appreciated. It's not just any gift; it's a symbol of the company's genuine eagerness to welcome them into their new role.

This welcome gift isn't merely about the physical item; it's a profound gesture that speaks volumes about the company's culture and values. It says, "The organization cares about you as an individual, not just as an employee." This seemingly small investment in a welcome gift holds immense potential to yield substantial returns in building trust, loyalty, and a profound sense of belonging.

But what makes a welcome gift truly special? It's the thought and intention behind it. It's about choosing an item that resonates with the company culture and reflects the warmth of the organization. Whether it's a personalized welcome letter, a company-branded notebook, or a token that signifies shared values, the welcome gift becomes a powerful symbol of the relationship between the new team member and the company.

Their experience from the very beginning shapes their perception of the organization they work for. Extending this personalized touch in the Pre-Onboarding stage, you help lay the foundation for a positive, memorable, and enriching journey.

Now, you're thinking about all that pesky paperwork, background checks, and the usual pre-employment stuff, right? I hear you, my friend; every company has to go through that drill. But here's the scoop – you can still make it less hassle for the new team member.

What's the secret? Well, it's all about having the right vendors in your corner. You want this process to be smooth sailing, not an obstacle course.

And hey, keeping the lines of communication wide open is the name of the game as well.

Sure, sometimes hiccups might pop up during this paperwork tango. Deadlines could shift, and things might get bumpy. But here's the deal – as long as you're talking with your new employee, explaining any curveballs, and ensuring they're cool with any changes, you're golden.

Now, I get it; some things are out of your hands. That's when you flip the script and show some genuine empathy. You can even get creative here. I've got this story for you – we had a candidate whose onboarding ride hit a few bumps. Paperwork was not going smoothly; you know how that goes.

But we didn't just sit around twiddling our thumbs. Our General Manager decided to step up. He picked up the phone, called his new employee, and said, "Hey, why don't you come over and join us for our company potluck? You don't need to bring a thing." And guess what? That candidate showed up and had a blast.

I'm not saying everything will fall into place like a perfectly orchestrated symphony every time, but get creative, my friend. When you offer someone a job, it's a sign you care about having them on your team. So, find ways to keep them onboard and avoid poachers from other companies.

In the next section, we will transition to the equally crucial stage of Orientation and Induction, where we focus on making the new team member feel valued and appreciated. We'll explore how a warm welcome and a special first-day surprise can set the tone for a remarkable first week and beyond.

Orientation and Induction (First Day and First Week)

The first day at a new job is akin to the opening chapter of a novel. It sets the tone for the entire story that follows. The goal during Orientation and Induction is to ensure that this chapter is one that the new team member will fondly remember.

Remember the perfect first day we discussed at the beginning of the chapter? This is where you put this into play. You want to make sure not only you, as the HR professional, greet the team member but also everyone from the hiring process and even the person they will be shadowing for their training is there to greet them. Some advice is to ensure these are organized days, even weeks before they start. That way, there will be no surprises for team members participating in the first-day meet and greet.

Now that the team member has gone through the first few hours of the day, you can start the orientation process. Orientation and Induction aren't just about the formalities of paperwork and company policies; they're about creating a memorable experience. It's about making someone feel like they're not just a worker but a valued member of the company community. This personal touch goes a long way in building a positive and lasting connection.

As the first week unfolds, continue to provide support and guidance to the new team member. Offer insights into the company's mission, culture, and values. Make sure to ensure they understand the workplace policies and procedures. And most importantly, encourage questions and curiosity.

The first week sets the tone for the new team member's integration into the organization. It's a time for them to absorb the company's ethos and start forming relationships. Combining a warm welcome with a special first-day gift aims to create a foundation of trust and belonging that paves the way for a successful journey ahead.

Training and Development (Initial 30 Days)

The first 30 days are pivotal for any new employee. It's a period of adjustment, learning, and adaptation. There is an investment in Training and Development tailored to their role.

Job-specific training is provided to equip them with the knowledge and skills they need to excel in their role from day one. Whether it's software proficiency, product understanding, or industry-specific insights, the Training and Development program is designed to empower them.

The training isn't a one-time event but an ongoing process that evolves with their needs. The new team member should be encouraged to ask questions, seek guidance, and participate in introductory workshops and seminars. It's an environment where curiosity and growth are allowed and encouraged.

During the initial 30 days, the focus is not just on what they can do for the company but also on what the company can do for them. They have the necessary tools, resources, and support to thrive in their new role.

The Training and Development process is more than just acquiring job-related skills. It's about personal growth and development. They are encouraged to set short-term and long-term goals and are provided with guidance and resources to help them achieve them.

Furthermore, the importance of continuous learning is emphasized. The commitment to the employee's growth doesn't end after the initial 30 days; it's an ongoing journey. Opportunities for skill enhancement, career development, and personal enrichment are provided.

Investing in their training and development ensures their success within the organization and fosters a sense of loyalty and commitment. It shows that there is care about their growth and advancement and that commitment is reciprocated in their dedication to shared goals.

Socialization and Integration (First Month)

Becoming part of a new team and organization can be exciting and daunting. The commitment during the first month is to ensure they feel like a cog in the machine and a valued community member.

Socialization and integration are critical components of the onboarding process. Facilitating introductions to colleagues and team members across different departments, arranging opportunities to meet and network with key stakeholders, and encouraging participation in team-building activities and company events—all contribute to building relationships, forging connections, and fostering a sense of belonging.   The workplace is not just a physical space; it's a community where individuals come together to achieve common goals. The commitment to their integration goes beyond lip service. Ongoing support and mentorship are provided to ease their transition. An environment is created where they can share their thoughts, ideas, and concerns without hesitation, and their progress in adapting to the company culture and values is monitored, recognizing that this journey is unique to each individual.

Fostering connections and building a sense of belonging ensures they don't feel like outsiders but are an integral part of the team. Opportunities for them to contribute their unique perspectives and ideas are provided, reinforcing the belief that every member's voice matters.

During this crucial first month, the focus is not only on helping them understand their role but also on helping them understand the organization's mission and vision. Encouragement is given to align their goals with the company's and to actively participate in the shared journey.

Workbook #3

Section 1: Reflective Comparison

Reflect on two contrasting onboarding experiences described: one negative and one positive. List the key differences in approach and outcome.

Section 2: Gifting Ideas

Think of 5 gift ideas for your company that also connects with your company. This gift will be sent to a new hire before their first day during the onboarding process. I will provide a few examples of a welcome box for a eco friendly company:

Gift Ideas

Eco Friendly Welcome Kit

Inside the welcome kit

- bamboo diary
- bamboo pen
- bamboo bottle
- wooden earphone organizer
- metal mobile stand

All products in this hamper are 100% plastic-free, chemical-free, cruelty-free

51

Section 3: Welcome Committee

Take the time to list every department within your organization. Next to each department, nominate a team member to serve as the Welcome Committee Leader. This individual's sole responsibility will be to take new team members in their department out for lunch or share a meal with them. Additionally, during this task, consider who will be in charge of ordering and paying for these lunches.

Section 4: Training and Development

Now it's time to use the department list you made in the previous section. I want you to write down each department again and coordinate meetings with the managers of those departments. You will ask them the last time they've update their SOP's/Training Manuals? next to the department. Any manual older than 2 years I want you to circle and follow up with those managers to make sure they are actually up to date. If not this is the perfect time to update them for your existing and especially future team members.

Team Building Activities

1. Escape Room
2. Office Trivia Game
3. Team Lunch Outing
4. Volunteer Day
5. Board Game Tournament
6. Workshop or Seminar
7. Outdoor Adventure Trip
8. Craft or Painting Session
9. Icebreaker Questions Session
10. Group Fitness Class
11. Cultural Exchange Day
12. Scavenger Hunt
13. Karaoke Night

Section 5: Socialization and Integration

Within the first 30 days, it's crucial to arrange one-on-one meetings between the new team member and each department manager, regardless of the department they're assigned to. Additionally, fostering a sense of camaraderie and connection is vital, which can be achieved through team-building activities outside of work hours, alongside other initiatives aimed at strengthening bonds. Below is a curated list of innovative ideas designed to enhance relationships between your new employee and the existing team. Please select the three ideas that resonate most with you and share them with your team for consideration.

4

Learning & Development

Make sure that team members know they are working with you, not for you.

- John Wooden

In the movie "Moneyball," inspired by the real-life story of Billy Beane and the Oakland Athletics, a memorable scene highlights a crucial leadership lesson. Here's the setup: Billy Beane, played by Brad Pitt, is the general manager of the Oakland A's, and Peter Brand, portrayed by Jonah Hill, is his assistant, shaking up the team's approach to player recruitment.

Now, let's dive into that scene. Beane and brand are finalizing a trade, and there's a player about to be traded. Typically, it's the GM's job to deliver the news, but Beane does something unexpected. He says, "Brand, it's your pitch. You break the news."

At first, the brand hesitates and feels nervous about delivering the news, as it's different from the usual play. But Beane stands firm. This move sends a clear message – Beane values the brand's insights, judgment, and shared ownership of its decisions. By having the brand personally convey the news, Beane underscores that they're a team, and each team member has a significant role in the organization's success.

This moment reflects Beane's leadership philosophy. He ensures team members know they're working with him, not just for him. Beane understands that genuine collaboration and shared decision-making responsibility lead to better outcomes. It's not about rigid hierarchy; it's about leveraging each team member's unique strengths and perspectives to achieve common goals.

In the world of business and leadership, this approach is golden. When employees feel invested in the company's success and actively participate in decision-making, they become more engaged, motivated, and committed. They're not simply following orders; they're taking the initiative, contributing their ideas, and taking ownership of the company's achievements and challenges.

Billy Beane's decision to empower Peter Brand to deliver the news during that trade is a powerful lesson in leadership and team dynamics. It reminds us that influential leaders cultivate an environment where team members feel like genuine partners and stakeholders, ultimately driving innovation and achieving remarkable results.

Continuous Learning and Education: Fueling the Growth Engine

Let's kick off this journey into the heart of development with a topic hotter than a Chicago summer – continuous learning and education. In today's fast-paced world, if you're not learning, you fall behind faster than a lead balloon.

Think about it this way: when cruising down the highway, you can't just park in the middle of the road and expect the world to wait for you. No, it would help if you kept moving forward, adapting to the changing terrain. The same goes for your and your team members' careers.

One thing you have to remember is that the world is constantly changing. New technologies, evolving customer expectations, and emerging trends are constant whirlwinds. If your team members don't keep up, they'll be left in the dust like yesterday's news.

I'm not saying your team members must be like Neo from "The Matrix," downloading new skills instantly. But they do need to be proactive about staying current. It's like being in a never-ending episode of a survival reality show. Adapt or get voted off the island – it's that simple.

You might think, "Alright, I'm on board with this continuous learning thing, but how do I make it happen?" Well, my friend, it starts with creating a culture as hungry for knowledge as a Chicagoan at a deep-dish pizza joint.

I will give you my top things to do to create a culture of continuous learning.

Lead by Example:

You can't expect your team members to embrace learning if you or their managers are stuck in your ways. Be the change you want to see. Show them that the company is committed to continuous learning by helping them and their managers pursue their development journey.

Provide Access:

Just like you would only send a soldier into battle with the right gear, don't send your team members into the ever-changing workplace without the necessary tools. Invest in their learning by providing access to online courses, workshops, and resources.

Encourage Exploration:

Remember when you were a kid, and everything was an adventure waiting to be explored? Encourage your team members to approach learning the same way. Let them explore topics that pique their interest, even if it's not directly related to their current role.

Celebrate Curiosity:

Curiosity is like a treasure map to learning gold. Celebrate and reward team members who ask questions, seek out new knowledge, and share what they've learned with others. It's like throwing fuel on the fire of curiosity.

Foster a Growth Mindset:

Encourage your team members to see challenges as opportunities for growth, not roadblocks. A growth mindset is like a superpower that helps them bounce back from setbacks and keep pushing forward.

Career Pathing and Progression: Navigating the Jungle of Ambition

Let's talk about something as important as knowing your way around the 'L' train in Chicago – career pathing and progression. It would help if you had a roadmap to navigate those bustling streets in the windy city. Well, your team members need a roadmap for their careers, too.

Picture this: you're on a road trip and cruising down Route 66. It's not just a random drive; you have a destination, a plan to get there, and exciting stops. That's what a career path is all about – having a clear destination and a plan to make the journey worthwhile.

When team members see a well-defined career path, they're more likely to stay engaged and motivated. It's like handing them a compass in the middle of a dense forest – they know where they're going and are excited about the journey.

I'm not saying you should promise instant promotions or raise expectations to the moon. Career pathing is about providing a roadmap that outlines the skills, experiences, and milestones needed to progress. It's like saying, "Here's the route; let's start the adventure."

So, how do you create these career paths that make team members as excited as a Sox fan at Guaranteed Rate Field? Let's break it down:

Set Clear Goals:

Work together with team members to set career goals. Where do they want to be in one year, five years, or even ten? Goals give them something to strive for and measure their progress against.

Identify Skills and Experiences:

Once you have the destination in mind, identify the skills and experiences required. It's like planning a hike – you need the right gear and training for the terrain ahead.

Map the Journey:

Lay out the steps needed to reach those goals. What roles, projects, or assignments will help team members gain the necessary skills? It's like plotting stops along a cross-country road trip.

Provide Support and Feedback:

Along the way, offer guidance and support. It's like being the co-pilot on this career journey. Regular feedback sessions help team members course-correct and stay on track.

Celebrate Milestones:

Remember to celebrate when they hit milestones. Recognizing their progress keeps them motivated and engaged, whether a small achievement or a big one.

Workbook #4

Five Stages of Training and Development

Section 1: Development Opportunities

Please list out all of your companies development opportunities. This includes education, workshops, and any other developmental opportunities team members can take advantage of.

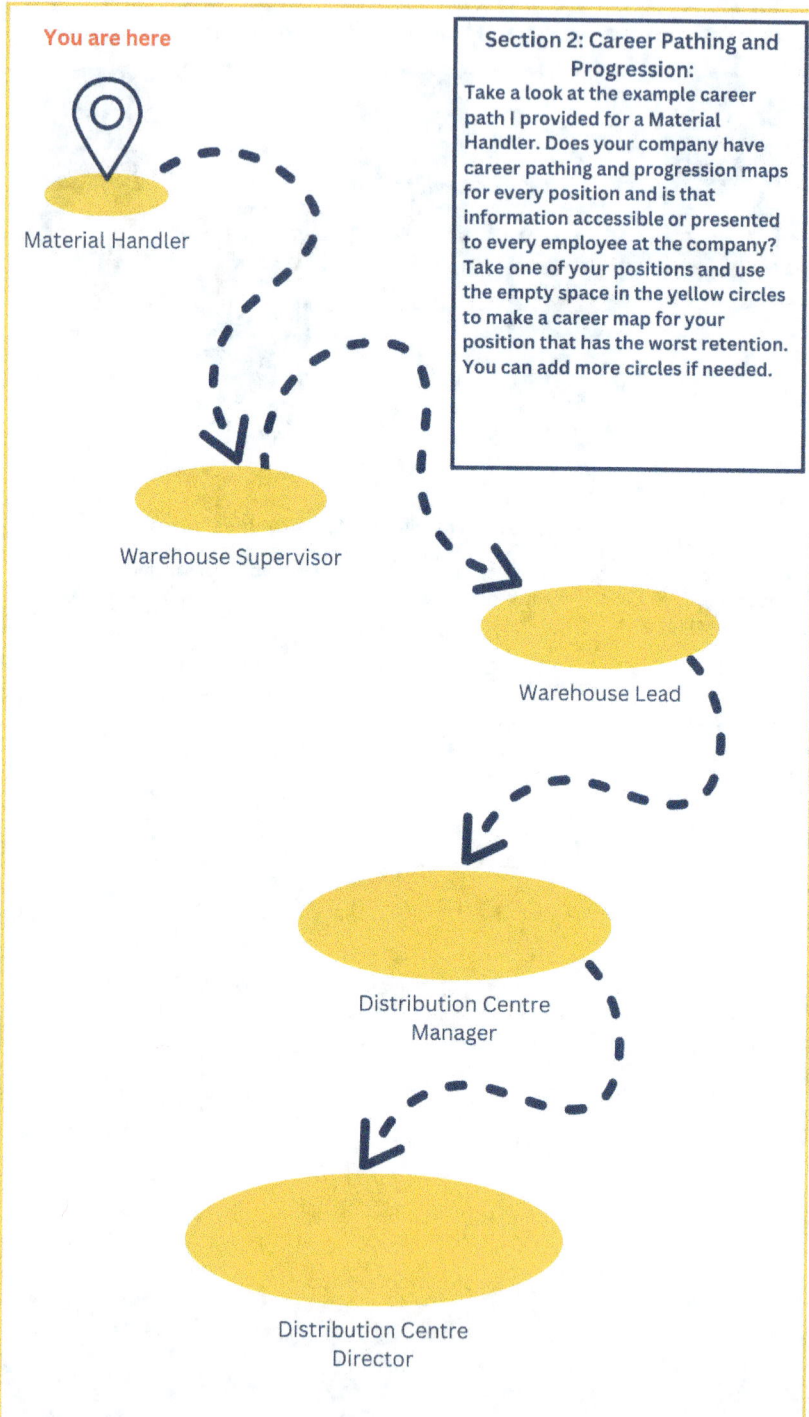

You are here

Material Handler

Section 2: Career Pathing and Progression:
Take a look at the example career path I provided for a Material Handler. Does your company have career pathing and progression maps for every position and is that information accessible or presented to every employee at the company? Take one of your positions and use the empty space in the yellow circles to make a career map for your position that has the worst retention. You can add more circles if needed.

Warehouse Supervisor

Warehouse Lead

Distribution Centre Manager

Distribution Centre Director

5
Recognition & Reward

Always treat your employees exactly as you want them to treat your best customers.

-Stephen R. Covey

Stephen Covey's wisdom is more relevant than ever in the fast-paced business world. How you treat your employees sets the tone for how they treat your customers. It's a simple equation, yet it packs a mighty punch in shaping your organization's success.

Now, for all the fans of "The Office" out there, you'll surely remember the episode "The Dundies." It's an absolute classic. But if you still need to get in the know, let me paint the picture for you.

Imagine Michael Scott, the head honcho at the Scranton branch of Dunder Mifflin, a guy known for his quirky antics and love for the unconventional. One day, he throws an awards ceremony unlike anything you've ever seen – The Dundie Awards. These weren't your typical accolades; we're talking categories like "Whitest Sneakers" and "Hottest in the Office." Michael seized the spotlight and owned the stage.

But here's the twist: as quirky and cringe-worthy as "The Dundies" were, they dished out a lesson that hits home—employee recognition is a big deal. In the world of Dunder Mifflin, it proved that even the zaniest gestures can go a long way in making your employees feel valued. It's a reminder that recognition sends a powerful message in all its quirky glory.

Unfortunately, not every workplace grasps this reality. In the real world, employees often clock in day after day, yearning for recognition, a fist bump, or even just a simple "thanks." Yet, for many, those affirmations never come. There are no awards ceremonies, raises, or words of appreciation from the higher-ups.

In these workplaces, the revolving door of turnover keeps spinning. Employees feel undervalued and underappreciated, prompting them to scout for better opportunities elsewhere. But what if we flipped the script? What if employers treated their team members like they do their best customers? What if every day at the office felt like "The Dundies," where hard work was celebrated, and recognition was just part of the package?

With the stage set, let's break down the Performance & Reward phase in the employee life cycle, starting with employee recognition.

Recognition & Rewards

Recognition and rewards are like the turbo boosters of motivation. They're the high-fives and victory laps that keep employees fired up. Employees crave acknowledgment for their hard work, and recognizing their contributions is a cornerstone of the Performance & Reward phase.

Recognition can take many forms, from a simple "thank you" to more formal awards. Effective recognition is timely and specific, highlighting the valued behaviors or outcomes. It reinforces positive actions and encourages employees to continue going above and beyond.

Conversely, rewards often have a tangible component, such as bonuses, promotions, or raises. While monetary rewards are essential, non-monetary recognition is equally valuable. Things like "Employee of the Month" awards, extra time off, or professional development opportunities can be powerful motivators.

The key to effective recognition and rewards is personalization. Understanding what motivates each employee and tailoring recognition to their preferences makes it more meaningful. Recognition and rewards should be consistent and tied to performance, creating a culture of appreciation and accomplishment.

Feedback & Communication

Open and honest communication is the heartbeat of the Recognition & Reward phase. Regular feedback is essential for helping employees understand how they're doing and what they can do to improve.

Feedback should flow in both directions, from managers to employees and vice versa. Managers should provide constructive feedback, highlighting areas of strength and suggesting areas for growth. Employees should feel comfortable sharing their perspectives, challenges, and ideas for improvement.

Effective feedback is specific, actionable, and focused on behaviors rather than personalities. It should be delivered promptly, not just during formal evaluations but also in day-to-day interactions.

In addition to feedback, communication should be transparent and informative. Employees should know how their performance contributes to the organization's goals and what opportunities for growth are available to them. A culture of open communication fosters trust and engagement, driving overall performance.

Employee Engagement

Employee engagement is the energy, enthusiasm, and dedication employees bring to work. Engaged employees are not just showing up for a paycheck; they're invested in the company's success.

During the Recognition & Reward phase, focusing on strategies that enhance employee engagement is essential. A highly engaged workforce is likelier to deliver exceptional performance, contribute innovative ideas, and stay loyal to the company.

Engagement strategies include fostering a positive company culture, promoting work-life balance, providing opportunities for involvement in decision-making processes, and creating a sense of belonging. Employee recognition and rewards also play a significant role in boosting engagement.

Regular feedback and communication are critical to keeping employees engaged. Managers should listen to their team members, address concerns, and actively seek their input on matters that affect their work.

Crafting a Culture of Appreciation: The Employee Recognition Game at Zappos

In the fast-paced world of online shopping, a company doesn't just sell shoes; they walk the talk when valuing their employees. I'm talking about Zappos, where shoes are just the story's beginning. It's a place where the spotlight shines on employee performance and recognition, and it's quite the show.

At Zappos, they kick things off with their "core values." These aren't just fancy words on a wall; they're the guiding principles that steer the ship. One of these values, "Build a Positive Team and Family Spirit," is their secret sauce.

Zappos takes a unique approach when it comes to recognizing great work. They've got this excellent currency called "Zollars." Employees use these Zollars to pat each other on the back for all sorts of achievements, no matter how small. And guess what? Zollars can be traded in for some seriously awesome rewards. It's like a game of recognition that everyone's winning.

But Zappos doesn't stop there. They throw these epic company-wide events and parties that are the stuff of legends. These shindigs aren't just about hitting milestones but celebrating the fantastic folks who make Zappos tick. It's like being part of an offbeat, lovable family.

When it comes to communication, Zappos doesn't believe in ivory towers. Former CEO Tony Hsieh used to hang out with employees from all levels. That kind of open-door policy makes everyone feel like they belong and motivates them to bring their A-game.

Zappos also has a thing for rewriting the rules. They've got this unique structure called "Holacracy," where employees can manage themselves and take charge of their roles. It's all about trust, and it sparks creativity and personal growth.

But it's not just about work; it's about well-being. Zappos offers fitness classes, mental health support, and stress-busting programs. They want their employees not just to be productive but also to be happy and healthy.

And here's the kicker: Zappos isn't just about making a profit; they're about giving back. They roll up their sleeves and get involved in their local community. They even encourage their employees to volunteer and make a positive impact.

If you ever thought those core values were just words, think again. Zappos dishes out "core value bonuses" to employees who embody these values. It's a nod to doing the right thing, and it's something that doesn't go unnoticed.

So, that's the scoop on Zappos. It's a place where performance and recognition aren't just policies but a way of life. It's a place where employees aren't just part of a team; they're part of a big, quirky family. So, next time you shop for shoes at Zappos, remember there's much more than just shoes in those boxes. Behind the scenes are employees who are celebrated, valued, and inspired to shine their brightest. That's the Zappos way, and it's nothing short of extraordinary.

Workbook #5

Section 1: Recognition Program Design:

Below, I have provided an example of a great way to show appreciation to your employees. This is called a recognition board, or some companies refer to it as a shout-out board. Take some time to design your own employee recognition program tailored to your company's needs.

Remember the 'Dundies' from The Office and how quirky and fun they were? Just like that, some employees at Dunder Mifflin enjoyed the Dundies. Keep in mind that you won't be able to please 100% of your staff, but it's far better to have 50% feeling appreciated than no one at all.

Ideas

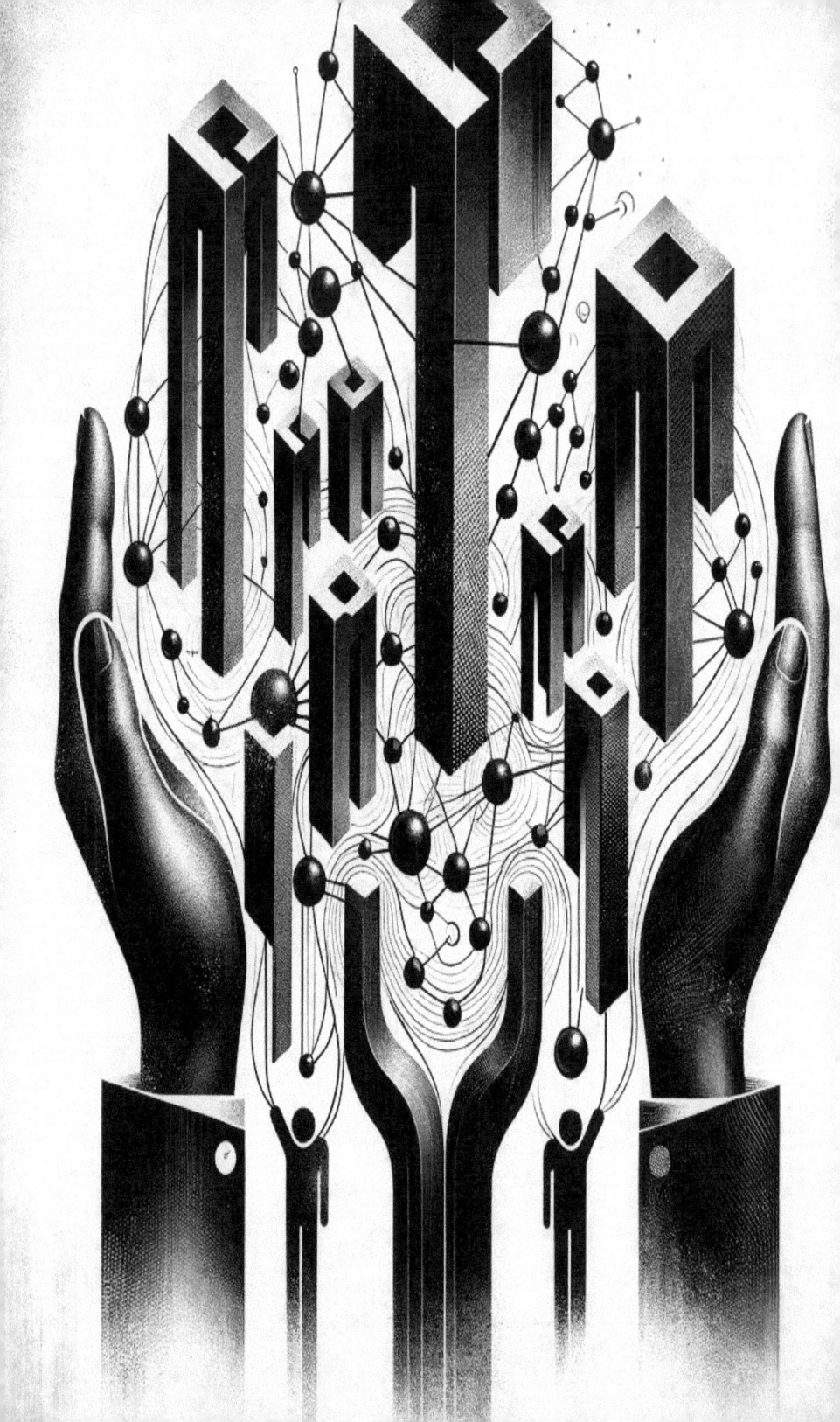

6
Retention

Your number one customer are your people. Look after employees first and then customers last.

- Ian Hutchinson

STOP THE PIZZA PARTIES!!

Remember those company pizza parties? They've been a go-to for ages, the classic way to try and boost employee spirits. Who doesn't love a slice of pizza, right? But here's the scoop: despite their popularity, these shindigs might not be as effective as you'd think when engaging employees. Here are some reasons why those company pizza parties might not be the engagement champs we wish they were:

Defining Employee Retention

Alright, let's break it down. Employee retention isn't just some fancy jargon; it's the lifeline of a thriving organization. It's about keeping your employees pumped, content, and committed to their roles within your company. Retention isn't just about preventing a workforce departure; it's about ensuring they're still passionate contributors to your company's mission.

The Importance of Retaining Top Talent

Now, why should you care about employee retention, you ask? Well, think of it this way: losing a top-performing employee is like losing the MVP from your championship-winning team. They've got skills, knowledge, and experience that are challenging to replace. High turnover can mess up the harmony of your workplace, messing with productivity, morale, and even customer satisfaction.

But it's not just about plugging holes; it's about creating a culture where your folks want to stick around and flourish. When your A-players see a future within your organization, they'll invest their time and energy into making your company a winner. It's a win-win situation.

The Cost of Employee Turnover

Employee turnover can have a significant financial impact on organizations. Understanding the cost of turnover is crucial for making informed decisions and implementing effective retention strategies. The formula to calculate the cost of employee turnover can vary depending on the specific factors and expenses you want to consider. However, here is a general formula that provides an overview of the cost calculation:

Cost of Employee Turnover = (Separation Costs + Replacement Costs + Training Costs + Lost Productivity Costs + Recruitment Costs)

Let's break down each component:

Separation Costs:

These are the costs of the employee's departure, including administrative tasks like exit interviews, paperwork, and processing final paychecks.

Replacement Costs:

These costs encompass the expenses related to finding a replacement, such as advertising job openings, agency fees, and background checks.

Training Costs:

When a new employee is hired, there are expenses associated with their training and orientation, including materials, training programs, and the time spent by trainers.

Lost Productivity Costs:

This category includes the decrease in productivity during the time it takes for the new employee to reach the same level of productivity as the departing employee. It can also cause productivity loss during the departure process.

Recruitment Costs:

These costs involve the expenses associated with recruiting and selecting the new employee, including HR staff time, job fairs, and recruitment events.

To get the total cost of employee turnover, you sum up all these costs and divide them by the total number of employees in your organization. This will give you the average price of turnover per employee. Remember that the specific costs and magnitudes can vary widely depending on the organization and industry.

Understanding the cost of turnover can serve as a wake-up call for organizations that underestimate its financial impact. It underscores the importance of implementing effective retention strategies to reduce turnover and associated costs. Now, let's delve deeper into the factors that impact retention and the plan to retain top Talent.

Career Development Opportunities

People want to grow and advance in their careers. They'll be eyeing other exit doors if they feel stuck at your company. Offering clear paths for career growth, plus training and development opportunities, can keep your employees excited about their future with your company.

Work-Life Balance

We all know that work shouldn't eat up your entire life. Maintaining a healthy work-life balance is vital for retention. Burnout is like the evil villain of employee loyalty. So, encourage time off, flexible schedules, and respect personal time. Your workforce will thank you.

Leadership and Management

Heads up, your employees don't just quit their jobs; they leave their bosses. Leadership is a massive deal when it comes to retaining employees. Great leaders inspire, support, and mentor their teams. But if you've got some not-so-great managers on your hands, they can drive employees away faster than you can say "exit interview." Solving leadership issues and training your managers is essential for retention.

Recognition and Rewards

Your employees want to feel appreciated. Regular recognition and rewards, from simple "thanks" to more formal pats on the back, can lift spirits and keep motivation soaring. When employees feel like their efforts matter, they'll stick around.

Employee Retention Strategies

So, where do we start? Building a positive culture is the foundation of retention. It begins with explicit values and a commitment to inclusivity, diversity, and respect. Encourage teamwork, communication, and a sense of purpose to make your workplace a spot where employees want to stay.

Competitive Compensation Packages

Offering competitive salaries and sweet benefits is a no-brainer. Keep an eye on your compensation structure, ensuring it aligns with your industry and location. Don't let top Talent slip away because of an uninspiring paycheck.

Career Progression and Development Plans

Help your employees chart their career paths within your organization. Offer training, mentorship, and chances for growth. Employees who see a future with your company are likelier to stick around.

Flexible Work Arrangements

Flexibility is a big deal nowadays, especially with remote work becoming a thing. Offering flexible schedules or remote work options can be a significant win for retention.

Employee Engagement Initiatives

Engaged employees tend to hang around. Invest in initiatives that boost engagement, like team-building events, volunteer opportunities, and wellness programs.

Mentorship and Coaching Programs

Pairing experienced employees with newcomers can help with onboarding and integration. Mentorship programs also provide valuable career guidance.

The Role of Leadership in Retention

Effective leadership is the key to employee retention. Ensure you have strong leaders in place and provide them with training and development opportunities.

Providing Leadership Training and Development

Leadership skills can be honed and developed. Leadership training can improve your managers' ability to retain their teams.

Leading by Example in Valuing Employees

Leaders set the tone for the organization. When leaders actively value and appreciate employees, it sends a powerful message throughout the company.

Recognizing and Addressing Leadership Challenges

Spot leadership challenges and address them pronto. Don't let ineffective or toxic leadership hurt your retention game.

Measuring and Monitoring Retention

Use metrics like turnover rate, tenure, and engagement scores to monitor retention. These stats can help you spot areas that need some TLC.

When employees head out the door, hold exit interviews to determine why they leave. This feedback can be a goldmine for improving retention.

Keep those lines of communication open with regular surveys and feedback channels. Act on employee feedback to address concerns and make retention even better.

Get nerdy with data analytics to find patterns and trends related to retention. Let data guide your decisions and make retention even smoother.

Southwest Airlines: Flying High with Employee Retention

Southwest Airlines is renowned for being a trailblazer in the airline industry regarding holding onto their valuable employees. They've got this exceptional way of treating their employees, including those friendly flight attendants, that really sets them apart. So, let's dive into the nitty-gritty of why Southwest Airlines is all the rage for having super-high employee retention and how their down-to-earth attitude towards their workforce plays a huge role in their bottom line.

What sets them apart is their one-of-a-kind, employee-centered culture. They don't just say it; they live and breathe it. Southwest Airlines puts its employees right at the center of everything they do. They believe that their success is all thanks to their fantastic workforce. So, from the ground crew to the cabin crew, everyone gets the VIP treatment.

Let's zoom in on those excellent flight attendants. At Southwest Airlines, they don't just see them as cabin staff; they see them as the real heroes of a smooth flight. They understand that these folks are critical players in ensuring passengers have a fantastic experience. So they give them the respect and recognition they deserve. When you know your work is valued, it's no surprise you'd want to stick around.

Remember, it's not just about pats on the back; it's also about the green stuff. Southwest Airlines knows that competitive compensation is a big deal. They're not just in the ballpark but hitting it out of the park. They offer attractive salaries and many benefits, like profit-sharing programs and those sweet travel perks. Who wouldn't want to work at a place where you can get paid while traveling?

Let's discuss numbers and why keeping employees happy at Southwest Airlines isn't just a warm and fuzzy feeling—it's a smart financial move. Remember that equation we talked about earlier? Well, let's run the numbers for Southwest.

Separation Costs:

These are the costs associated with the departure of an employee. It includes exit interviews, administrative work, and final payments or settlements. Let's assume an average separation cost of $2,000 per flight attendant.

Replacement Costs:

These costs are related to recruiting and onboarding a new flight attendant. They encompass advertising, screening, interviewing, and hiring expenses. On average, this cost can be around $5,000 per new hire.

Training Costs:

Training costs include expenses for initial training and orientation for new flight attendants. This can involve classroom training, safety training, and other related expenses. For this calculation, let's consider an average training cost of $3,000 per flight attendant.

Lost Productivity Costs:

When a flight attendant leaves, there may be a period of decreased productivity as new hires get up to speed. Let's assume an average lost productivity cost of $2,500 per flight attendant.

Recruitment Costs:

These costs include advertising job openings, interviews, and other recruitment-related expenses. On average, this cost can be around $1,000 per flight attendant.

Now, let's put these numbers into our trusty equation:

Cost of Employee Turnover for Flight Attendants =

($2,000 + $5,000 + $3,000 + $2,500 + $1,000)

Cost per employee = $13,500

When you crunch those numbers, you'll find that losing just one flight attendant at Southwest Airlines can be a whopping $13,500. Yes, you read that right! That's the financial hit they take whenever someone decides to take off.

Imagine if they didn't prioritize their employees, didn't treat their flight attendants like the stars they are, and had a revolving door of departures. Those costs would add up fast and could seriously dent their bottom line. It's not just about valuing their employees for the sake of it; it's also a pretty smart financial strategy. High employee retention helps them dodge these hidden costs and keeps their operation running smoothly.

Workbook #6

Section 1: Cost of Employee Turnover Calculation

Use this worksheet to calculate the cost of employee turnover within your organization for your biggest turnover position. Input your specific costs in the fields provided to gain a better understanding of the financial impact.

Separation Cost :

Administrative tasks (exit interviews, paperwork, etc.): $
Processing final paychecks: $
Other separation costs (specify): $

Separation Cost Total:

Replacement Costs:

Advertising job openings: $
Agency fees: $
Background checks: $
Other replacement costs (specify): $

Replacement Costs Total:

Training Costs:

Initial training and orientation: $
Training materials: $
Training programs: $
Time spent by trainers: $
Other training costs (specify): $

Training Costs Total:

Lost Productivity Costs:

Decrease in productivity during the transition period: $
Lost productivity during the departure process: $
Other lost productivity costs (specify): $

Lost Productivity Costs:

Recruitment Costs:

HR staff time: $
Job fairs and recruitment events: $
Other recruitment costs (specify): $

Recruitment Costs Total:

Separation Costs
Replacement Costs
Training Costs
Lost Productivity Costs
Recruitment Costs

Total Cost of Employee Turnover =

Section 2: Retention ROI Analysis

Use this worksheet to calculate the Return on Investment (ROI) for implementing specific retention strategies within your organization. Follow the steps and provide the necessary data to assess the financial impact of reduced turnover costs and improved productivity.

Step 1: Identify Costs and Savings

Total Costs Incurred for Implementing the Retention Strategy

Training costs: $
Implementation costs (e.g., software, resources): $
Other costs (specify): $

Total Costs Saved Due to Reduced Turnover

Separation costs savings: $
Replacement costs savings: $
Lost productivity costs savings: $
Recruitment costs savings: $
Other turnover-related cost savings (specify): $

Step 2: Calculate Net Savings from the Retention Strategy

Net Savings = (Total Costs Saved) - (Total Costs Incurred)

Step 3: Calculate Return on Investment (ROI)

ROI (%) = [(Net Savings) / (Total Costs Incurred)] x 100

Results:

Total Costs Incurred Implementing Retention Strategy: $
Total Costs Saved Due to Reduced Turnover: $
Net Savings from the Retention Strategy: $
Return on Investment (ROI): %
Productivity Improvement Benefits: [Description]

Other Intangible Benefits: [List of Benefits]

Step 4: Assess Additional Benefits

Productivity Improvement Benefits:

Describe any improvements in productivity resulting from the retention strategy implementation (e.g., increased efficiency, reduced errors).

Other Intangible Benefits:

List any other intangible benefits (e.g., improved employee morale, enhanced company reputation).

Step 5: Analysis and Conclusion

ROI Analysis:

Analyze the calculated ROI. Is it a positive or negative ROI? Interpret the ROI results in the context of the retention strategy's effectiveness.

7
Offboarding

Talent is the multiplier. The more energy and attention you invest in it, the greater the yield. The time you spend with your best is, quite simply, your most productive time.

— Marcus Buckingham

Imagine a couple in a long-term relationship who, after much consideration, decide to part ways. They sit down together, have an open and honest conversation about their feelings, and express gratitude for their time together. They acknowledge each other's contributions and agree to part on amicable terms.

In a similar vein, an excellent offboarding process mirrors this upbeat breakup. It involves clear communication and planning between the departing employee and the organization. The employee can share their reasons for leaving and are met with understanding and appreciation. The organization expresses gratitude for the employee's contributions and helps them navigate the transition with professionalism and empathy.

During a good breakup, both parties part ways on favorable terms. The organization acknowledges the employee's achievements, provides necessary support, and ensures a smooth handover of responsibilities. This approach opens the door for future interactions, such as alum engagement, referrals, or a potential company return. It reinforces the organization's reputation as a considerate employer.

Imagine a couple going through a messy breakup filled with arguments, hurtful words, and misunderstandings. They avoid communication, refuse to acknowledge each other's feelings, and part ways with bitterness and resentment.

In contrast, a destructive offboarding process can be likened to this tumultuous breakup. It lacks effective communication and support for the departing employee. The organization may disregard the employee's contributions or fail to acknowledge their departure. This neglect can lead to negative feelings, such as frustration, disappointment, or unfulfilled closure.

During a bad breakup, there needs to be a plan in place to ensure a smooth transition of responsibilities, leaving both the organization and the departing employee in disarray. This approach burns bridges and can lead to alienation, making it unlikely for the former employee to engage positively with the organization post-departure.

The offboarding phase of the employee life cycle can be compared to good and bad breakups, highlighting the importance of a considerate and well-managed offboarding process. A good offboarding experience fosters positive feelings, maintains connections, and allows for potential future engagement, while insufficient offboarding expertise can lead to negative emotions and severed ties. Therefore, organizations should strive to make employee departures as amicable and respectful as possible to preserve relationships and reputation.

The Importance of Offboarding

Remember that "talent is the multiplier. The more energy and attention you invest, the greater the yield. The time you spend with your best is, quite simply, your most productive time." In talent management, the offboarding process is the final act in nurturing and respecting that Talent. The chapter closes the book on an employee's journey within an organization. While often overshadowed by its counterpart, onboarding, and offboarding are essential to the employee lifecycle.

Planning and Preparation

A successful offboarding process doesn't happen by chance; it requires meticulous planning and preparation. Just as a couple contemplating separation must weigh their options and anticipate the challenges of living apart, organizations must strategize for employee departures. This includes creating policies, procedures, and guidelines for a seamless offboarding experience.

The Offboarding Process

The offboarding process should be a well-structured series of steps that guide the organization and the departing employee through the transition. Much like an amicable breakup conversation, it involves clear communication and mutual understanding. Here are the critical components of an effective offboarding process:

Exit Interviews

Exit interviews are the heart of the offboarding process. They provide departing employees a platform to express their reasons for leaving and share their experiences. These candid conversations offer valuable insights to help organizations improve employee retention strategies.

Return of Company Property

Like returning personal belongings after a breakup, departing employees must return company property. This includes office keys, access cards, electronic devices, and other assets issued during their tenure.

Final Pay and Benefits

Ensuring the departing employee receives their final paycheck, including any accrued vacation or leave balances, is crucial. It's a matter of fairness and legality.

Transitioning Responsibilities

Just as a couple dividing their shared possessions must ensure a fair distribution, organizations should facilitate a smooth handover of responsibilities. This involves identifying a successor or a temporary replacement and providing adequate training and support.

Farewell and Gratitude

Expressing gratitude is a hallmark of an upbeat breakup. Organizations should acknowledge the departing employee's contributions, celebrate their achievements, and bid them farewell with sincerity.

Legal and Compliance Considerations

Navigating the legal landscape is an essential aspect of offboarding. It involves adhering to employment laws, ensuring compliance with non-disclosure agreements, and addressing any potential legal matters arising from the departure.

Offboarding Best Practices

Effective offboarding goes beyond mere procedure; it encompasses best practices that foster a respectful and supportive environment. These practices include creating a comprehensive offboarding checklist, maintaining open communication with remaining employees, preserving positive relationships, ensuring data security, and facilitating knowledge transfer.

Technology and Offboarding

In today's digital age, technology plays a pivotal role in offboarding. It involves revoking access to company systems, retrieving company-issued devices, and safeguarding sensitive data. Properly leveraging technology can streamline the offboarding process and enhance security.

Continuous Improvement and Feedback

Just as relationships benefit from post-breakup reflection, organizations should seek feedback from departing employees to continuously improve their offboarding process. Feedback mechanisms and surveys can help identify areas for enhancement.

Offboarding in a Remote Work Environment

With the rise of remote work, offboarding has taken on new dimensions. Organizations must adapt their offboarding procedures to accommodate remote employees, ensuring a smooth transition despite physical distances.

Offboarding Challenges and Solutions

Recognizing and addressing common offboarding challenges, such as emotional distress, knowledge gaps, and potential security risks, is essential. Solutions to these challenges help organizations navigate the offboarding process more effectively.

The Role of Offboarding in Employer Branding

The way an organization handles offboarding impacts its employer brand. A positive offboarding experience can lead to alumni engagement, referrals, and an enhanced reputation as an employer.

Workbook #7

Section 1: Resignation and Retirement offboarding

When an employee puts in a resignation or plans to retire this is a time to celebrate your employees. Just because someone put in their resignation doesn't mean you should dismiss them right away. You never know what skills that person may gain from another company and could be valuable for your future leadership positions. I will give you a few offboarding party examples:

Set up an interactive display
Create a guest book table where attendees can leave a personal message for the celebrant. Include a display with photos of the employee, along with any awards and other accolades they received during their time on the job.

Trivia
Host a trivia contest about the retiree. Include workplace-related questions, like what they kept on their desk, what they liked to listen to while they worked, or their favorite afternoon pick-me-up snack or coffee drink. Hand out prizes to those who answer the most questions correctly.

Ideas

Section 2: Offboarding Checklist

Use this checklist to ensure a smooth offboarding process for departing employees. Customize the checklist by adding or removing items as needed to align with your organization's specific offboarding procedures.

Employee Information:

Exit Interviews:

Returning Company Property:

Final Pay and Benefits:

Transitioning Responsibilities:

Feedback/Continuous Improvement:

Legal Considerations:

- Employee Name:
- Department/Team:
- Supervisor/Manager:
- Contact Information (for follow-up):

- Schedule an exit interview with employee.
- Prepare a list of questions on their experience.
- Share feedback with relevant departments for process improvement.

- Retrieve office keys and access cards.
- Collect company-issued electronic devices (laptop, phone, tablet, etc.).
- Ensure the return of security badges, parking permits, or other access-related items.

- Calculate the final paycheck, including any accrued vacation, leave balances, or bonuses.
- Provide information on the timeline for receiving the final paycheck.
- Explain the process for returning any excess reimbursement or benefits overage.

- Review and complete all legal paperwork
- Ensure compliance with employment laws.
- Address any non-disclosure agreements

Section 2 (Continued): Create your offboarding Checklist

Conclusion
Shaping the Future of HR

Can you believe we've made it to the final chapter of our adventure? Let's take a moment to look back at our path, from attracting Talent to saying farewell to our teammates during offboarding. It's been quite the rollercoaster ride.

Setting Realistic Goals and Expectations

Implementing new strategies within an organization is a delicate process, filled with challenges and opportunities. Recognizing the importance of setting realistic goals and expectations cannot be overstated, as it lays the foundation for successful change management. We will go over the necessity of adopting a strategic, phased approach to ensure not only the adoption of new processes but also their sustained impact over time.

Understanding the Scope of Changes

Before diving into the implementation, it's crucial to understand the full scope of proposed changes. This understanding aids in assessing your organization's readiness and capacity for change, ensuring that initiatives are not just well-intended but also feasible and aligned with current capabilities.

Prioritizing Initiatives

Prioritizing initiatives is a critical step in the implementation process. Criteria for prioritization should include the potential impact on organizational goals, required resources, and overall feasibility. Initiatives should be rolled out in phases, starting with those that promise quick wins to build momentum and demonstrate value early in the process.

Gaining Buy-In

Achieving buy-in from employees and management alike is essential for the success of any change initiative. Effective strategies include maintaining open lines of communication, ensuring transparency in decision-making, and fostering an inclusive environment where feedback is valued and considered. For management, aligning the initiatives with your organization's strategic objectives and demonstrating potential ROI can secure the necessary support.

Developing an Implementation Roadmap

A detailed implementation roadmap (Gantt chart), complete with timelines, milestones, resource allocation, and assigned responsibilities, guides the organization through the change process. This roadmap should be flexible, allowing for adjustments based on ongoing feedback and evolving conditions, ensuring the organization can adapt as necessary.

Example Gantt chart

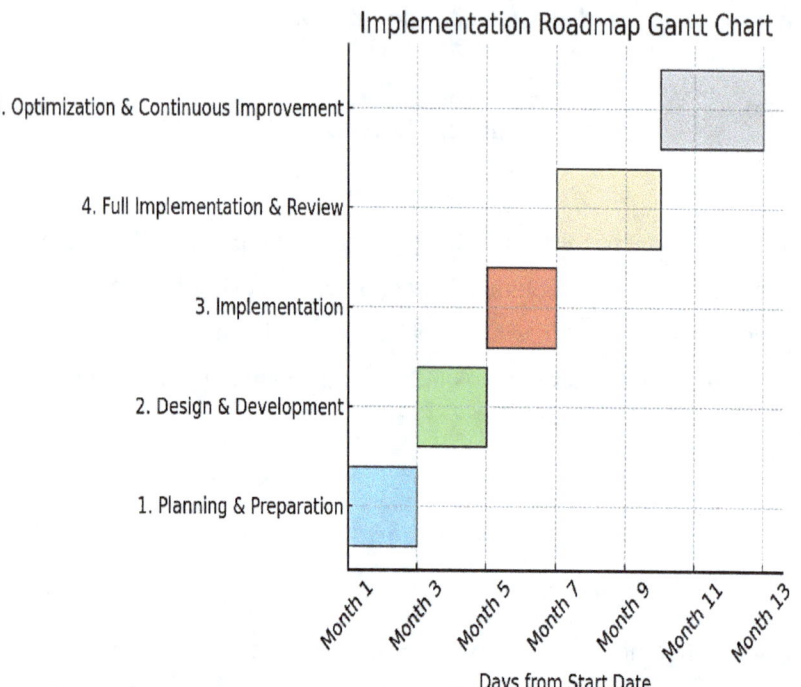

Keeping track of progress against predefined goals is crucial. This not only allows for real-time adjustments but also fosters a culture of continuous improvement. Success should be measured not just by the immediate outcomes but also by the long-term impact and the organization's ability to adapt and grow.

Setting realistic goals and strategic prioritization are the cornerstones of successful implementation. By embracing a culture of continuous improvement and adaptability, organizations can navigate the complexities of change, ensuring that new strategies are not only implemented but also integrated into the fabric of the organization, leading to sustained growth and improvement.

I am here to provide a roadmap for you and your organization looking to implement change effectively. By focusing on realistic goals, prioritization, and stakeholder engagement, the path to successful change becomes clearer and more attainable.

Closing Thoughts

In closing, remember this: breaking the revolving door cycle isn't just about holding onto talent; it's about creating a workplace where everyone is appreciated, supported, and fired up to bring their A-game. Leadership and teamwork are our guiding stars, propelling us toward a future where the organization and its champions thrive.

We're wrapping up this incredible journey with heartfelt thanks for sharing it. As you step into the world of HR armed with newfound knowledge and determination, remember that you can shape a future where the revolving door becomes a relic and the gates to success swing wide open for all.

About the Author

Raymond Williams III stands as a distinguished figure in the realm of Human Resources (Talent Acquisition), bringing an unparalleled depth of expertise and insight to recruitment.

Boasting countless years of hands-on experience, Raymond has left an indelible mark on the HR/Talent Acquisition landscape, particularly through his remarkable contributions to Fortune 500 companies. His tenure in the industry is characterized by the innovative recruitment processes he has designed, which have not only enhanced the operational efficiency of these organizations but have also set new benchmarks for HR excellence. Raymond's work has been pivotal in shaping the strategic direction of HR departments, ensuring they align with the overarching goals and values of the organization.

Beyond his strategic contributions, Raymond is also deeply committed to nurturing the next generation of Talent Acquisition professionals. He has taken under his wing numerous new recruiters across a variety of sectors, imparting to them the knowledge, skills, and wisdom accrued over his illustrious career. Through his mentorship, Raymond has fostered a culture of continuous learning and professional growth, empowering his protégés to excel in their roles and contribute meaningfully to their organizations.

Raymond is a visionary leader whose work continues to influence the field of Human Resources profoundly. Through his innovative strategies, commitment to mentorship, and unwavering belief in the power of human potential, Raymond has truly redefined what it means to lead with empathy and intelligence in the modern workplace.

Resources

Discover more about my workshops and the unique insights I offer by utilizing the link below. Additionally, let's connect on LinkedIn for further collaboration and networking opportunities: (https://www.linkedin.com/in/raymond-williams-iii-7085311a3/)

Workshop Info:

https://drive.google.com/file/d/1YxtkDht0JKBux4KdrstFqidMvjwzJGpg/view?usp=drive_link